LET ME WRITE THIS DOWN...

JUDITH K JACOBS

What is a poem but emotions,
Words of strength, weakness,
love, laughter or sorrow.
A soul in print from beginning
To end.
Dreams of a lifetime; a role
created,
a role played.

DEDICATIONS

Judith Kay Jacobs was born in Bemidji, Minnesota on March 14, 1942. The family moved to Fergus Falls, Minnesota in 1945. Judy began reading at five years old. She began writing At 23 and is still writing At 82. Judy has worked in many capacities at Grace United Methodist Church plus enjoying music as a handbell soloist. She was also church secretary at St. James' Episcopal Church for 16 years. In between, she enlisted in the U.S. Army and is a veteran.

Judy and her late husband, Franklin, had four children: Bethany, Todd, Jeff and Sue plus many grandchildren: Kayla, Mariah, Alex; grandchildren Keagan, Jasmine, Ava, Maddie, Alexus and Blade, to whom this book is dedicated.

DUST (A LITTLE RELIGION)

The sun is hot,
casting not a shadow on me as
Father…

dust swirls around my feet
and I slowly move forward

dragging my robe through it,
sandals tearing on rough pebbles.

Sweat and blood drip into my
eyes, into the dust
Father…

as hands reach out to help me
only to be pushed back,

voices inside me, around me
weeping, crying out…help them!
Father!

The sky darkens.
Yes, my Son, I hear you.
I'm Coming!

An Ending

Before I close my eyes for good

I maybe shall or wish I could

hold you tight and brush your cheek,

kiss your lips...your warmth I seek.

Memories flow, we love once more,

I want to stay – it's hard to go.

I know...I know.

Still, God's breath feels like early spring.

I feel His presence, hear angels sing.

So, I must leave you on your own

until on that breath, you'll find your home.

SILENCE

Silence can be deafening.
Then cries split the air;
cracked the pond.
Nothing moved in the world
as children cried and died.
Where is joy...
There is silence.
There is war.

Passion

inspire me with a look.

A look that fills my heart

with spring flowers.

lean against me

and I will hold you

with thoughts of caring,

thoughts of tenderness.

Only you can feel the love in my soul.

It's Over

I can rest without you,
as you can plainly see.
I'm sorry, I don't love you.
It is not meant to be.

Your arms are open, eager.
Your eyes are bright with tears.
I'm sorry, I don't love you,
It's my emotion that you fear.

I have other memories
I can't live without.
I'm sorry I don't love you
but I have no doubt.

I don't care if you need me,
for you I am not right.
I know your heart is breaking,
but now I'll say, "Goodnight."

THE CHILD

Did you see the hungry child in the street?

Did you see the tears...in this country?

Did the child go home at the end of the day

or was home the box in the alley...

Did the child's head rest on soft pillows

in love or concrete?

You know... when you are hungry, do you cry?

PLEASE STAY

Don't leave me my love.
I want you to stay.
Don't die, please don't die,
I need you today.
I've loved you so long,
for so many years.
We've laughed and we've talked
through all our fears.
We've walked through the park
hand-in-hand, you, and I
enjoying our time...
please come back, don't die...
No! Don't leave me, don't leave me!
oh, I love you so much!
Stay with me, my darling,
I need your gentle touch
Just one more day.
I can't let you go.
One more kiss, love.
Wait for me... I know.

Heartbreak

The sun shines brightly.

The table is set for coffee and fun...

my friend has come!

As she sits across from me

we talk of good times we've had together,

when I notice her black eye...What?

Did you take a turn and fall?

She shook her head, shed a tear...

I looked at her in constant dread,

"Don't tell me he,"... she cried some more.

It really shocked me to the core.

"I know a lawyer, we'll see him now,"

and grabbed my keys, drove into town.

She talked to someone who made sense.

He went to jail at his expense.

Heartbreak there was, there was no turning back.

Defend yourself as you can from any attack.

Believe me, he knew he was in error.

That Religion…

I wonder often why I am tied to religion.

When I was 1 (I remember my crib),

I would sit and watch the curtains move

in the open window, pine trees waving.

An empty rocking chair would move.

I felt someone was there. Scared? No.

When I was six, I would not sleep

but look out of the window

watching the stars in the evening sky.

I did not feel alone. Scared? No.

I did the same thing constantly growing up

and always felt the same.

Now I feel a presence when I enter any Church…

Serene.

Caring.

Love.

Wonder…

I know He is there.

Leaving

The nursing home lights are dim, hiding a starry sky.

Morphine takes its toll on you as you lie

dreaming of long ago, a hundred years of life.

We turn you to your side and hear your weary sigh.

Then we saw you raise your hand and heard your cry,

"Mama, Mama, I don't want to die."

He takes you by the hand, and you pass by.

How Many...

How many times have you kissed me, hugged me?
How many times have you kissed me, hugged me?
God knows.
How many times have you screamed at me,
degraded me?
God knows.
How many times did you threaten
our babies, to kill them if I did not do as you said?
God knows...
He also understands insanity.
God saved me.

DEATH

When you died, I didn't feel you left.

There was movement in the trees.

The casket lowered in the ground

amidst the twirling leaves.

I walked slowly down the road

and felt you by my side.

My spirit lifted for a moment,

a feeling I cannot deny.

I saw you in my mind's eye,

heard your laughter in the air.

Saw you walking across a field,

sun touching your golden hair.

You were always helping others

toward a life they hoped to lead.

You always asked with purpose

if there was anything they'd need...

Now you hunt and fish once more

on God's majestic shore.

Wind blows across the Prairie
winding through wheat and corn alike.

Willows wave, then slowly bow down
leaves dancing together left then right.

Fall has come, the kids are playing,
frost covers the silo in the night.

The old farmhouse, two stories standing
wait for children who used to play...

a family had once gathered together
at a table where they loved to pray.

MODERN CRUCIFIXION

do you see me?

I am nine, ten, eleven, twelve…

Who played dodgeball, baseball, basketball, football, soccer.

I like hunting fishing water skiing dirt biking snowboarding hockey

I like computers

do you see me

I run to school fast - someone is behind me.

There it is!

Up the steps, down the steps

to my classroom at the end of the hall.

Someone is waiting.

I can feel it.

I sit at my desk and pretend I'm invisible.

I am alone.

My friends tripped me on the way to school,

slammed me into the wall in the hallway,

spit on me called me names…

are you the same friends I used to play with?

I'm afraid to go to the bathroom.

I'd like to hide inside my desk —

could I really, really fit?

You rammed me hard on the playground.

I fell.

Adults asked you if you were all right,

but left me on the ground.

Why doesn't anyone hear when you yell over and over,

"you're stupid… you're dumb… retard, retard, retard and more

Teacher, why don't you listen?

You walk away.

Don't you see my sadness, my fear, my tears?

How would you feel?

What would Jesus say?

sometimes in the night
I feel alone.

The stars watch,
the moon waits.

I am still alone.

It's darker than usual,
the shadows are quiet.

I am alone.
I wait for the sun.

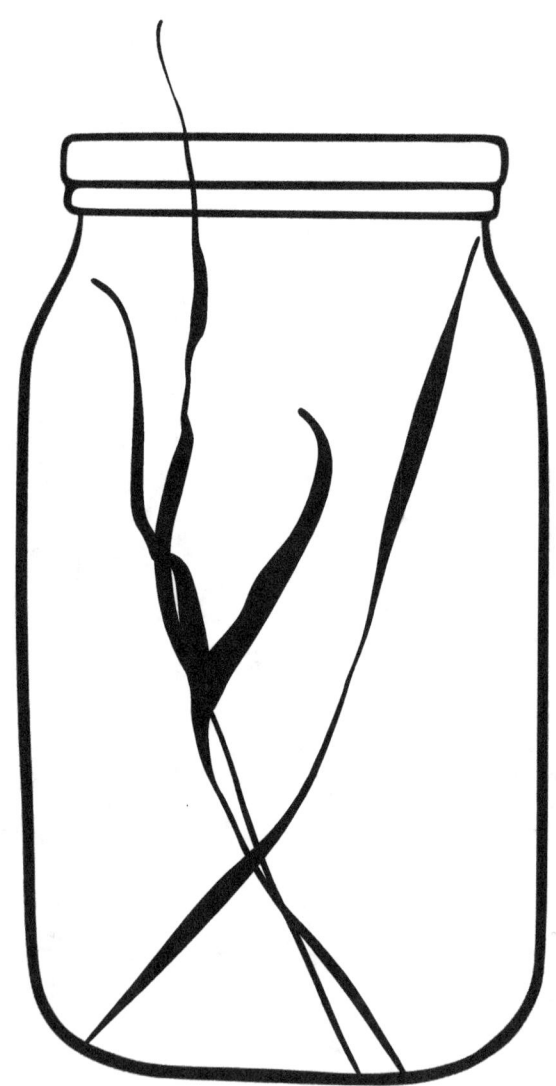

You were buried today.

I stand here looking at your beautiful tombstone...your name, dates.

Tears flow as memories rise. I will miss you my love...always.

Until we meet again, and dance in the moonlight...

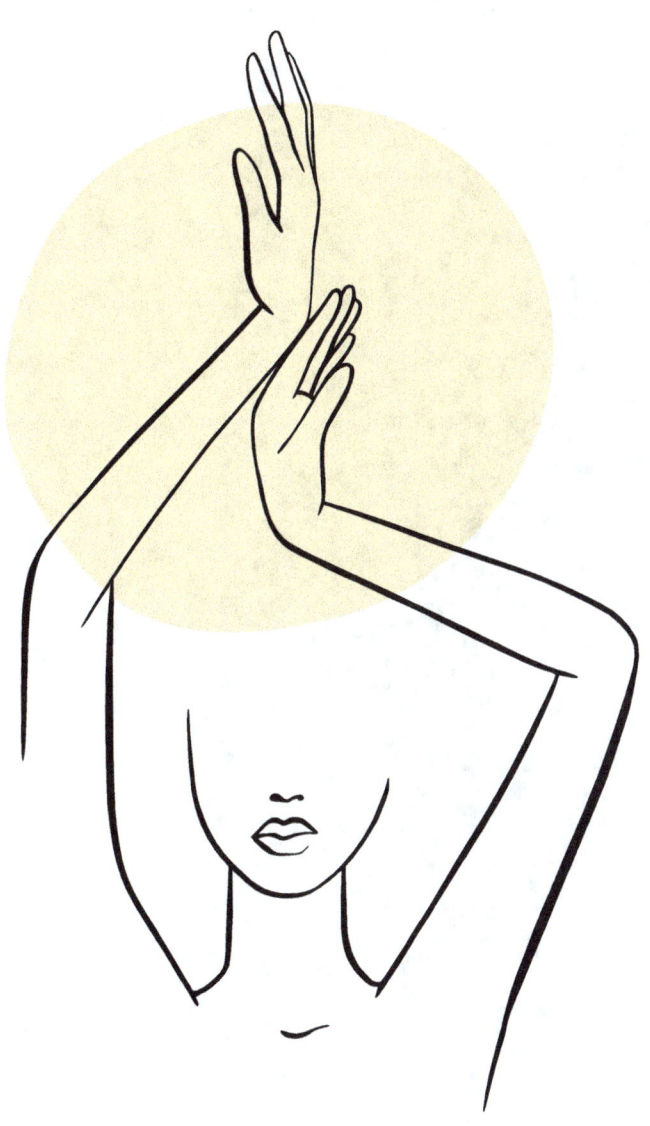

I slept close to you last night.

So lovely, pure delight.

I listened to your soft breathing in the morning light.

Birds called to us from a distance,

A curtain moved softly in the breeze.

My fingers touched your face in love.

a bank of water cascades a road
up in an arch so fine,
droplets floating through the air
spraying cliffs in rhythmic time
whirlpool form deep and wide
caressing trees, shores and loop
searching for the ebbing tide
moving through the fog

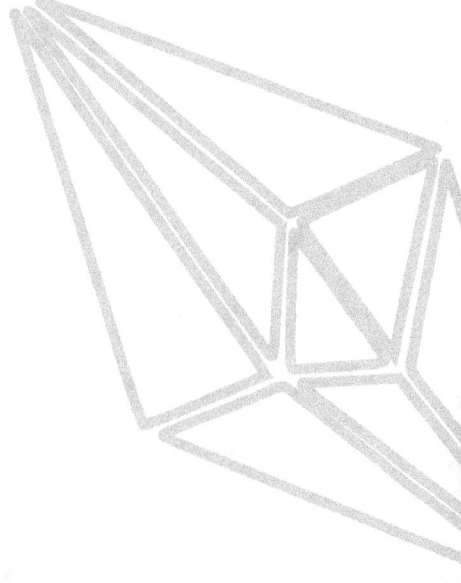

the anchoes up

the boat is gone

the summertime's at end-

it won't be long

before leaves dance

in cool lake air

and geese are flying

everywhere!

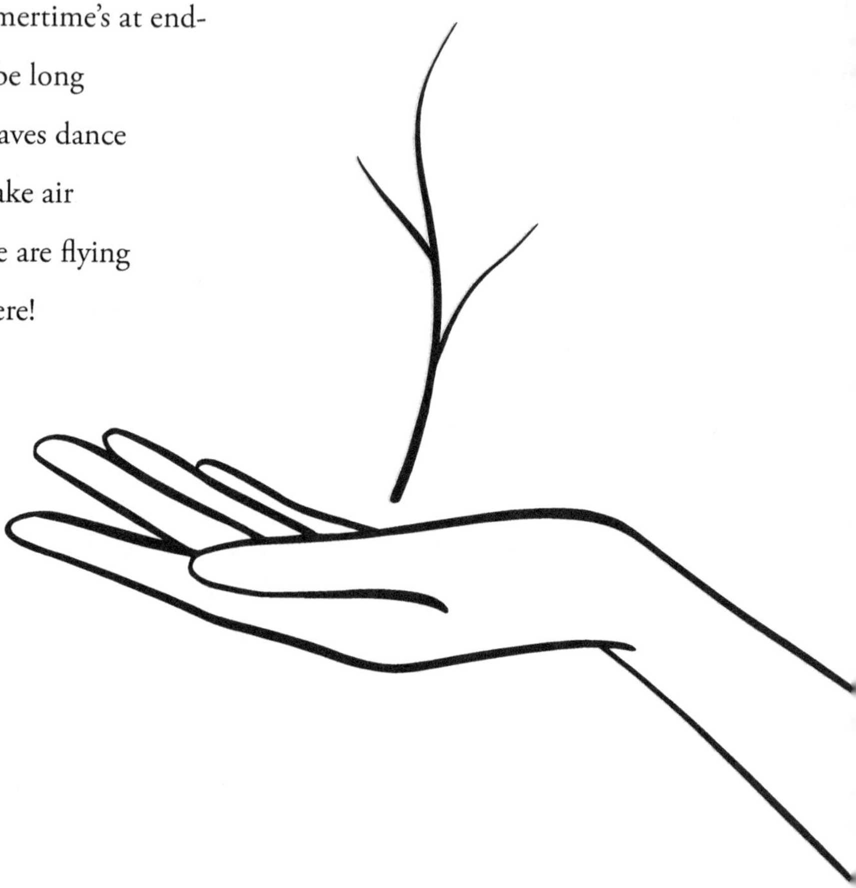

One foot at a time

Move forward

What's wrong?

You can do it, can't you?

Focus on something.

The tallest tree in the forest…

One rain drops…

Impossible?

You have the power,

Only you have the courage.

One foot at a time.

Days...

Days of mist,
days of fire.
Days of bliss
like no other.

Days of frost,
days of loss.
Days of tears
like no other.

Days of light,
days of dark.
Days of sun,
like no other.

Days of hate,
days of love.
Days of fate,
like no other.

Days of play,
days of rest.
Days of blessings,
like no other.

Wet snow fell all night
covering green lawns
like a warm blanket.

Branches hang heavy
brushing piles of snow
to the ground.

Red Cardinals grace
a snow-covered fir tree,
a striking contrast

groups of colorful finches
gather at a feeder
for an early breakfast.

Deer join them together
for food and water
at the nearby pond.

Winter has arrived

As You Died,

trees whispered,

a call to swirling leaves.

then it snowed,

your ashes moving instead.

I walked up path

feeling your presence,

my spirit and your spirit were one.

your laughter was carried

through fields,

then you were gone.

LIFE HAS ITS TWISTS AND TURNS,

sometimes earthshaking,

sometimes not.

We count our blessings-

caress, talk, love.

We can have trouble and suffering,

But we learn to prevail.

REVEREND

I know you are God's voice,

vows were taken, you made a choice.

To Him only you do belong and for many years you've sung His song. You would walk and pray in sun or rain though some roads were paved in pain. The light around you never dims as long as you have love for Him.

Let your beauty haunt me,

I am yours and you are mine.

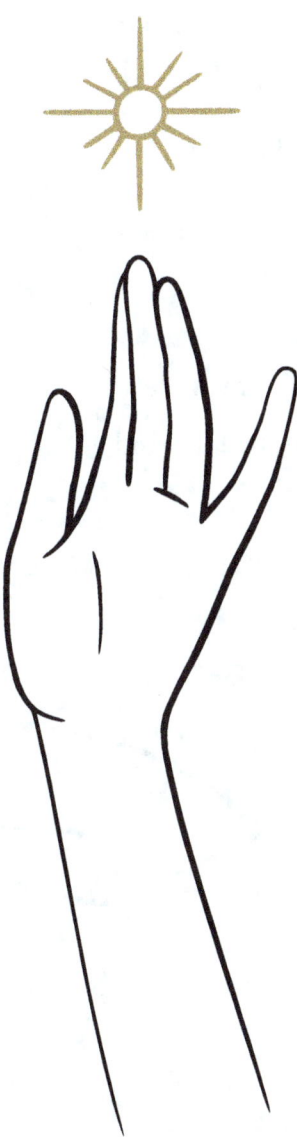

Not Death

I did not die,

and where the ground is cold

I will not lie.

My body's encased in pure, white gold

and my soul has learned to fly.

My soul is where our Lord directs;

near Him by the sea.

I glide the skies

and touch the stars,

which He made for you and me.

I pass o'er mountains built by His hand

and cover the desert with ease.

I sing by the brook,

a dove circles above,

and dance beneath bright-leafed trees.

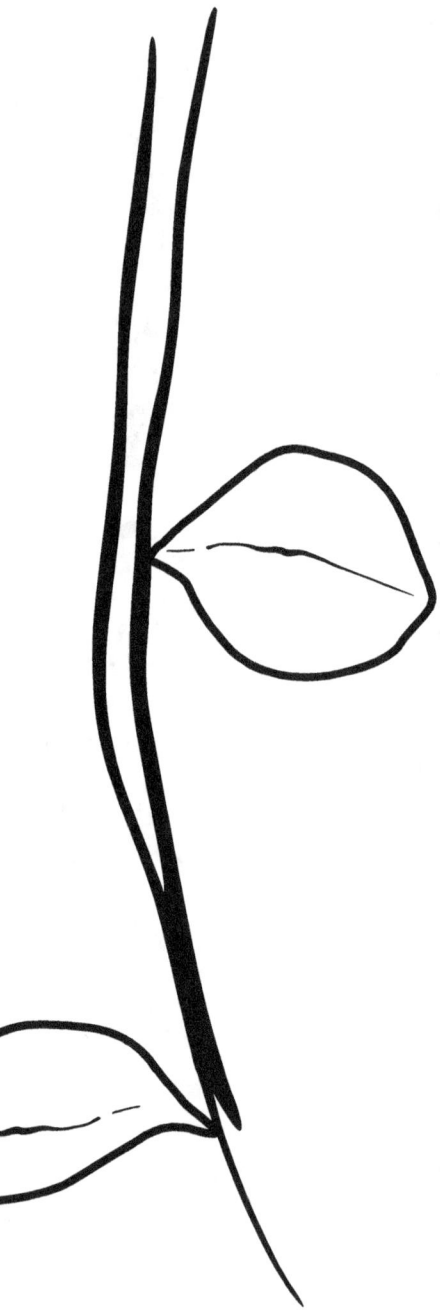

My sins, turned to stars
He wiped away with a sigh,
His gentle hand covered by brow.
A smile from our Lord
is a rainbow to you,
and peace is within me now.
Don't cry, don't cry
for a soul is reborn
to the Father and Son of our earth.
I have found that in death
we love even more,
and are pure in the joy of rebirth.

About the Author

Judith Kay Jacobs was born in Bemidji, Minnesota on March 14, 1942. The family moved to Fergus Falls, Minnesota in 1945. Judy began reading at five years old. She began writing At 23 and is still writing At 82. Judy has worked in many capacities at Grace United Methodist Church plus enjoying music as a handbell soloist. She was also church secretary at St. James' Episcopal Church for 16 years. In between, she enlisted in the U.S. Army and is a veteran. Judy and her late husband, Franklin, had four children: Bethany, Todd, Jeff, and Sue plus many grandchildren: Kayla, Mariah, Alex; grandchildren Keagan, Jasmine, Ava, Maddie, Alexus, and Blade, to whom this book is dedicated.

www.ingramcontent.com/pod-product-compliance
Lightning Source LLC
Chambersburg PA
CBHW060144150626
46550CB00014B/1331